westermann

W0281549

NOTTING HILL GATE

Grammatiktrainer 5

Notting Hill Gate 5
Grammatiktrainer

Materialien zu Notting Hill Gate 5

Für Lehrkräfte

- Textbook für Lehrkräfte 5 (ISBN 978-3-14-128284-9)
- Materialien für Lehrkräfte 5 (ISBN 978-3-14-128294-8)
- Lernerfolgskontrollen 5 (ISBN 978-3-14-128320-4)
- CD für Lehrkräfte 5 (ISBN 978-3-14-128304-4)
- DVD für Lehrkräfte 5 (ISBN 978-3-14-128314-3)
- Online-Diagnose zu Notting Hill Gate 5
  www.onlinediagnose.de

Für Schülerinnen und Schüler

- Textbook 5 (ISBN 978-3-14-128200-9)
- Workbook 5 (inkl. Audios) (ISBN 978-3-14-128210-8)
- Interaktive Übungen 5 (WEB-14-128220)
- Arbeitsbuch Inklusion 5 (inkl. Audios)
  (ISBN 978-3-14-128230-6)
- Klassenarbeitstrainer 5 (ISBN 978-3-14-128246-7)
- Wortschatztrainer 5 (ISBN 978-3-14-128240-5)
- Westermann Vokabeltrainer-App zu Notting Hill Gate 5
  www.westermann.de/vokabeltrainer

Das digitale Schulbuch und digitale Unterrichtsmaterialien für Schülerinnen und Schüler und für Lehrkräfte finden Sie in der BiBox – dem digitalen Unterrichtssystem passend zum Lehrwerk. Mehr Informationen über aktuelle Lizenzen finden Sie auf www.bibox.schule.

www.westermann.de/nhg

westermann GRUPPE

© 2022 Westermann Bildungsmedien Verlag GmbH, Braunschweig, www.westermann.de

Das Werk und seine Teile sind urheberrechtlich geschützt. Jede Nutzung in anderen als den gesetzlich zugelassenen bzw. vertraglich zugestandenen Fällen bedarf der vorherigen schriftlichen Einwilligung des Verlages. Nähere Informationen zur vertraglich gestatteten Anzahl von Kopien finden Sie auf www.schulbuchkopie.de.
Für Verweise (Links) auf Internet-Adressen gilt folgender Haftungshinweis: Trotz sorgfältiger inhaltlicher Kontrolle wird die Haftung für die Inhalte der externen Seiten ausgeschlossen. Für den Inhalt dieser externen Seiten sind ausschließlich deren Betreiber verantwortlich. Sollten Sie daher auf kostenpflichtige, illegale oder anstößige Inhalte treffen, so bedauern wir dies ausdrücklich und bitten Sie, uns umgehend per E-Mail davon in Kenntnis zu setzen, damit beim Nachdruck der Verweis gelöscht wird.

Druck A[1] / Jahr 2022
Alle Drucke der Serie A sind im Unterricht parallel verwendbar.

Redaktion: Doris Bos, Emma Klimczak und Annika Kulling
Illustrationen: Ulf Marckwort, Kassel
Umschlaggestaltung: LIO Design GmbH, Braunschweig
Layout: LIO Design GmbH, Braunschweig
Druck und Bindung: Westermann Druck GmbH, Braunschweig

ISBN 978-3-14-**128386**-8

Liebe Schülerin, lieber Schüler,

„Hilfe, Grammatik!“ – denken sicherlich viele von euch, denn Grammatik hat einen schlechten Ruf und manche haben sogar richtig Angst davor. Aber ohne Grammatik – die Regeln zur Bildung oder Verwendung einer Sprache – könnten wir uns alle nicht sinnvoll und gut verständlich unterhalten. Wir alle benutzen ständig unbewusst Grammatikregeln in unserer Muttersprache.

Grammatik kann sogar richtig Spaß machen. Das glaubst du nicht? Dann schau dir die vielen Übungen in diesem Heft an! Sie werden dir dabei helfen, zum Grammatik-Profi zu werden!

Jedes Kapitel beginnt mit einem Einführungstext, in dem die Strukturen, um die es geht, vorkommen. Dann werden sie in einem „Grammar Help“-Kasten erklärt, und dann sollst du selbst als „Language Detective“ auf Spurensuche gehen. Danach gibt es Übungen zu diesem Thema.

Die Lösungen für die „Language Detective“-Aufgaben  und für alle Übungen kannst du dir hier herunterladen: **www.westermann.de/128386**.
Es ist wichtig, dass du deine Ergebnisse der „Language Detective“-Aufgabe mit den Lösungen vergleichst, bevor du die Übungen machst. Nur so weißt du vorher schon, ob du auf der richtigen Spur bist. Nach dem Lösen der Übungen vergleichst du am besten alles noch einmal.

Wenn du die Grammatik gut beherrschst, wirst du dich auf Englisch sicher ausdrücken können.

Wir wünschen dir viel Spaß und Erfolg bei der Arbeit mit diesem Grammatiktrainer!

Über diesen QR-Code gelangst du auf die Webseite
www.westermann.de/128386
Dort findest du alle Lösungen und Grammatik-Videos (**DIGITAL+** video).

Unsere Lerntipps:

Karteikarten

Karteikarten haben eine praktische Größe und lassen sich überall mit hinnehmen.
Schreibe dir wichtige Erklärungen zur Grammatik auf Karteikarten. Notiere dir Formen oder Regeln und ein paar Beispielsätze.

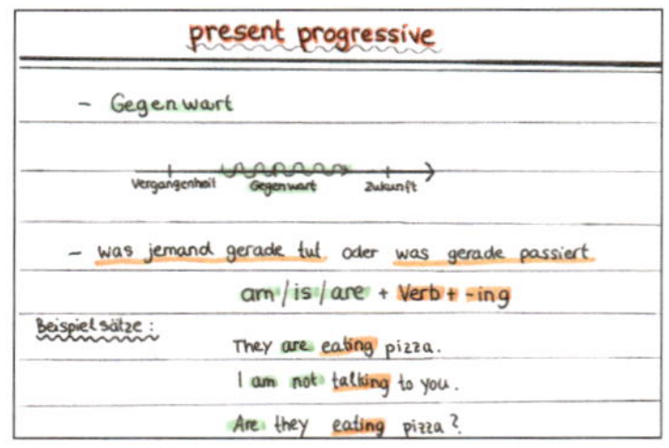

Der richtige Ort zum Lernen

Es ist nicht gut, am gleichen Ort zu lernen, an dem man sich ausruht, also auf dem Bett oder dem Sofa. Richte dir einen möglichst bequemen Platz ein, an dem du nicht abgelenkt bist. So kannst du dich besser konzentrieren.

Pausen sind wichtig

Auch beim Lernen zu Hause sind Pausen extrem wichtig. Dein Gehirn kann nur eine gewisse Anzahl an Informationen auf einmal abspeichern, danach braucht es eine Ruhezeit.
Es ist wichtig, dass du in den Pausen etwas Wasser trinkst und vielleicht auch etwas isst. Das hilft deiner Konzentration.

Gemeinsam lernen

Es ist gut, sich Zeit zum konzentrierten Lernen alleine zu nehmen.
Gemeinsames Lernen ist aber auch sehr effektiv und für viele Menschen motivierender als alleine zu lernen. Du kannst mit Klassenkameraden oder auch mit Mitgliedern deiner Familie lernen. Erkläre ihnen doch einmal, was du gerade lernst, oder lass dich von ihnen abhören.

Und natürlich hilft es, immer wieder zu üben – aber das tust du ja bereits mit diesem Grammatiktrainer! ☺

Introduction

Hello!

My name is Hannah. I'm eleven years old. I'm from Notting Hill in London. This is my cat Blacky. Her eyes aren't green, they are very special. One eye is brown and one eye is blue.

My brother James is fifteen. He's a football fan. He isn't here now. Sam and Ben are my best friends. They're twins. They're big rock music fans. I am not a rock music fan, I'm a hip hop fan.

Grammar Help

DIGITAL+ video 28

Be ist das englische Verb für „sein". Es gibt drei Formen: ***am, are*** und ***is***. Es gibt auch Kurzformen, die du beim Sprechen und in persönlichen E-Mails und Chats verwenden kannst.
Bei der Verneinung verwendest du ***not*** oder ***n't*** (z. B. ***aren't***).

Personalpronomen	Langform	Kurzform	Verneinung	Beispiel
I	**am**	I**'m**	**am not / 'm not**	I **am** from London.
you, we, they	**are**	you**'re** / we**'re** / they**'re**	**are not / aren't**	You **are** from London.
he, she, it	**is**	he**'s** / she**'s** / it**'s**	**is not / isn't**	She **is** from London.

Language Detective

a

Underline all the forms of the verb *be* in the introduction text.
Use different colours: red for *am*, blue for *are* and green for *is*.
Circle all the forms with "*not*".
Unterstreiche alle Formen des Verbs *be* im Einführungstext.
Verwende unterschiedliche Farben: Rot für *am*, Blau für *are* und Grün für *is*.
Kreise alle Formen mit „*not*" ein.

b

Circle the right verb form. Kreise die richtige Verbform ein.

1 My cat **is / are** very sweet.

2 I **are / am** eleven years old.

3 My name **is / am** Hannah.

4 James **am / is** my brother.

5 We **are / is** from Notting Hill.

6 Notting Hill **is / are** in London.

7 They **is / are** my best friends.

8 He **am / is** a rock music fan.

Make a picture

1

Colour the words in the correct colour. **Male die Wörter in der richtigen Farbe aus.**

1 braun: das englische Wort für ***„du“***
2 gelb: die Form von ***be***, die zu ***I*** gehört
3 blau: das englische Wort für ***„sie“***
4 grün: die Form von ***be***, die zu ***they*** gehört
5 rot: die Form von ***be***, die zu ***it*** gehört
6 grau: das englische Wort für ***„wir“***

be	be	I	he	be	he	he	be	be	I
be	he	he	is	be	I	I	he	it	it
it	I	is	is	is	I	he	it	be	I
I	is	is	is	is	is	he	it	it	he
is	is	is	is	is	is	is	I	are	he
I	am	am	am	am	am	be	are	are	are
it	am	am	am	she	am	be	are	are	are
it	am	we	am	am	am	he	he	you	it
it	am	we	am	am	am	he	I	you	it

People

2

Look at the photos. Match the sentence parts. **Sieh dir die Fotos an. Verbinde die Satzteile miteinander.**

1

2

3

4

5

6

1 She
2 You
3 They
4 I
5 He
6 It

A isn't small.
B am from London.
C aren't twelve, you're thirteen.
D is my brother.
E are at school.
F isn't happy.

1	*F*
2	
3	
4	
5	
6	

I'm eleven years old

3

Complete the sentences with the short forms.
Vervollständige die Sätze mit den Kurzformen.

1 I am eleven years old. ⇨ *I'm* ________ eleven years old.
2 You are my best friend. ⇨ ________ my best friend.
3 We are not from Manchester. ⇨ ________ from Manchester.
4 He is not very nice. ⇨ ________ very nice.

Adam

4

Read the notes about Adam. Write sentences. Use the long forms of *be*.
Lies die Notizen über Adam. Schreibe Sätze. Verwende die Langformen von *be*.

1. twelve years old
2. not from London
3. from Nottingham
4. not a rock music fan

1 Adam ______
2 ______
3 ______
4 ______

Benisha

5

Complete the sentences with the right forms of *be*.
Vervollständige die Sätze mit den richtigen Formen von *be*.

am · ~~is~~ · are · am · are · is · is · are

My name _is_ Benisha. I ______ from Germany and I ______ eleven years old.

My brother ______ eleven, too. We ______ twins. He ______ a basketball fan.

Our mum and dad ______ great. They ______ very funny.

Over to you

Write a text about yourself. Look at number 5 for help. You can add more ideas.
Schreibe einen Text über dich. Sieh dir als Hilfe Nummer 5 an. Du kannst weitere Ideen hinzufügen.

Hello,

My name ______. I ______ from ______.

I ______ years old. My ______ years old.

My hobbies ______ and ______.

______

Introduction

Hello! My name is Millie. I have got two little twin brothers and I've got a baby sister. We've got a big house with a small garden. We've got a cat, her name is Molly. She has got blue eyes. We've got a dog, too. His name is Henry.

My brothers have got a big bedroom. They have got two beds. They have got lots of toys, but they haven't got posters. I have got a small room. I haven't got a desk.

Grammar Help

DIGITAL+ video 29

Have got ist ein Verb und heißt auf Deutsch „haben". Bei ***he***, ***she*** und ***it*** verwendest du ***has got***. Auch für ***have got*** und ***has got*** gibt es Kurzformen. Die Verneinung bildest du mit ***not*** oder den Kurzformen ***haven't*** und ***hasn't***.

Personalpronomen	Langform	Kurzform	Verneinung	Beispiel
I, you, we, they	**have got**	**'ve got**	**have not got / haven't got**	I **have got** a dog.
he, she, it	**has got**	**'s got**	**has not got / hasn't got**	He **has got** a dog.

Language Detective

a

Underline all the forms of the verb *have got* in the introduction text.
Circle all the forms with "*not*".

Unterstreiche alle Formen des Verbs *have got* im Einführungstext.
Kreise alle Formen mit „not" ein.

b

How do you say that in English? Find the forms in the introduction text.

Wie sagt man das auf Englisch? Finde die Formen im Einführungstext.

1 Ich habe: ______

2 sie hat: ______

3 wir haben: ______

4 sie haben: ______

5 sie haben nicht: ______

6 ich habe nicht: ______

Tom and his friends

1

Circle the right form of *have got*. Kreise die richtige Form von *have got* ein.

1 Tom **has got / have got** a cat.

2 They **has got / have got** a big house.

3 I **has got / have got** a skateboard.

4 He **hasn't got / haven't got** a sister.

5 We **haven't got / hasn't got** a pet.

6 I **'ve got / 's got** a new football.

7 You **haven't got / hasn't got** a guitar.

8 She **have got / has got** two rabbits.

They have got …

2

Look at the pictures. Write sentences with *have got* or *has got*.
Sieh dir die Bilder an. Schreibe Sätze mit *have got* oder *has got*.

1

2

3

4

1 He ______________________ a guitar.

2 They ______________________ phones.

3 They ______________________ a dog.

4 She ______________________ a brother.

Alex

3

What has Alex got? What hasn't he got? Write sentences.
Was hat Alex? Was hat er nicht? Schreibe Sätze.

1 Alex ______________________

2 ______________________

3 ______________________

4 ______________________

She's got a skateboard

4

Complete the sentences with the short forms of the verb *have got*.
Vervollständie die Sätze mit den Kurzformen des Verbs *have got*.

1 She has got a skateboard. ⇨ *She's got* ______ a skateboard.

2 I have got a guitar in my room. ⇨ ______ a guitar in my room.

3 We have got two rabbits. ⇨ ______ two rabbits.

4 They have got a small house. ⇨ ______ a small house.

5 He has got lots of books. ⇨ ______ lots of books.

6 You have not got a dog. ⇨ ______ a dog.

7 She has not got homework today. ⇨ ______ homework today.

8 I have not got a brother. ⇨ ______ a brother.

Over to you

Write a text about what you have and haven't got. The words in the box can help you.
Schreibe einen Text darüber, was du hast und was du nicht hast. Die Wörter im Kasten können dir helfen.

brother · sister · desk · lots of books · dog · rabbit · guitar · skateboard

I've got ______

Introduction

Paul: Hi, nice to meet you. What's your name?
Olivia: My name is Olivia. And who are you?
Paul: I'm Paul. Are you from London?
Olivia: No, I'm not. I'm from Bedford.
Paul: Is Bedford nice?
Olivia: Yes, it is. Where are you from?
Paul: I'm from London. Are you eleven?
Olivia: No, I'm not. I'm twelve. Are you eleven?
Paul: Yes, I am.

Grammar Help

DIGITAL+ video 28

Willst du mit dem Verb ***be*** (= sein) Fragen bilden, stellst du ***am***, ***is*** oder ***are*** an den Satzanfang.

Entscheidungsfrage	Kurzantwort
Am I your friend?	Yes, you are. / No, you aren't.
Is Ben from London?	Yes, he is. / No, he isn't.
Are they hungry?	Yes, they are. / No, they aren't.

What, ***where*** und ***who*** sind Fragewörter. Willst du eine Frage mit Fragewort stellen, stellst du das Fragewort an den Satzanfang.

Frage	Antwort
What is your name?	My name is Bülent.
Where is he from?	He is from London.
Who is your best friend?	My best friend is Lisa.

Language Detective

a

Underline all the questions in the introduction text. Circle the forms of the verb *be* in the questions.
Unterstreiche alle Fragen im Einführungstext. Kreise die Formen des Verbs *be* in den Fragen ein.

b

Circle the right word. Kreise das richtige Wort ein.

1 **What / Who** is your name?
2 **Is / Are** you from London?
3 **Am / Is** Bedford nice?
4 **Are / Is** you eleven?
5 **Where / What** are you from?
6 **What / Who** are you?

Scrambled questions

1

Unscramble the questions and write them down.
Bringe die Fragen in die richtige Reihenfolge und schreibe sie auf.

1 are – Where – from – you – ? ______
2 hungry – they – Are – ? ______
3 Who – that – is – ? ______
4 you – ready – Are – ? ______
5 your – friend – Am – I – ? ______
6 Are – from – London – they – ? ______
7 we – Brighton – from – Are – ? ______
8 there – many – Are – playgrounds – ? ______

Questions to a new friend

2

Complete the questions with the words from the box.
Vervollständige die Fragen mit den Wörtern aus dem Kasten.

Are · Is · Is · Are · is · are · is · Is · Are

1 What ______ your name?
2 Where ______ you from?
3 Who ______ your friend?
4 ______ your brothers at home?
5 ______ your dog in the garden?
6 ______ your friends at your school?
7 ______ your guitar blue?
8 ______ your skateboard new?
9 ______ your brothers eleven and twelve years old?

Yes, I am

3

Read the answers first. Then write the questions. Lies zuerst die Antworten. Schreibe dann die Fragen.

1 *Are you eleven years old?* ______ Yes, I am eleven years old.

2 ______ Yes, my family is from England.

3 ______ No, they aren't from London.

4 ______ No, he isn't a music fan.

Hello!

4

Fiona is helping Lisa to write a message to Ben from Leeds. Write down the sentences in English.
Fiona hilft Lisa, eine Nachricht an Ben aus Leeds zu schreiben. Schreibe die Sätze auf Englisch auf.

Beispiel: Lisa: Wie sage ich, dass ich zwölf Jahre alt bin? Fiona: *I'm twelve years old.*

1 Lisa: Wie frage ich, ob Leeds groß ist?

Fiona: ______

2 Lisa: Wie frage ich, ob er ein Fußballfan ist?

Fiona: ______

3 Lisa: Wie frage ich, ob Mustafa sein Freund ist?

Fiona: ______

Over to you

Your class has new email partners in a school in England. Which questions do you ask a new friend? Write them down.
Deine Klasse hat neue E-Mail-Freunde in einer Schule in England. Welche Fragen stellst du einem neuen Freund / einer neuen Freundin? Schreibe sie auf.

What ______

______

______

Introduction

Emma: You've got a sweet dog. I love dogs! I'm Emma.
Ben: Hi, I'm Ben and this is Taco. Have you got a dog, too?
Emma: No, I haven't. I've got two rabbits.
Ben: That's nice! Have they got a big cage?
Emma: Yes, they have. They've got a very big cage.
Have you got brothers or sisters?
Ben: No, I haven't. Have you got brothers or sisters?
Emma: Yes, I have. I've got four sisters and three brothers.
Ben: Oh, that's a lot! Have you got a big garden to play in?
Emma: Yes, we have.

Grammar Help

DIGITAL+ video 29

Willst du mit dem Verb ***have got*** (= haben) Fragen bilden, stellst du ***have*** oder ***has*** an den Satzanfang.

	Entscheidungsfrage	Kurzantwort		Entscheidungsfrage	Kurzantwort
	Have I got my phone?	Yes, you have. / No, you haven't.		**Have** we got a rabbit?	Yes, we have. / No, we haven't.
Singular	**Have** you got a garden?	Yes, I have. / No, I haven't.	**Plural**	**Have** you got a brother?	Yes, we have. / No, we haven't.
	Has he/she/it got a toy?	Yes, he/she/it has. / No, he/she/it hasn't.		**Have** they got a house?	Yes, they have. / No, they haven't.

Language Detective

a

Underline all the forms of *have got* in the introduction text. Circle all the forms of *have got* in the questions.
Unterstreiche alle Formen von *have got* im Einführungstext. Kreise alle Formen von *have got* in den Fragen ein.

b

Circle the right word. Kreise das richtige Wort ein.

1 **Have / Has** you got a dog?
2 **Have / Has** your rabbits got a big cage?
3 **Have / Has** your house got a garden?
4 **Have / Has** your brother got a hamster?

Many questions

1

Unscramble the questions and write them down.
Bringe die Fragen in die richtige Reihenfolge und schreibe sie auf.

1 you – got – Have – cat – a – ? ______

2 we – homework – Have – got – ? ______

3 got – your family – a big – Has – house – ? ______

4 Sarah – a new – Has – schoolbag – got – ? ______

5 you – got – Have – computer – a – ? ______

6 they – a – Have – got – dog – ? ______

More questions

2

Complete the questions with the words from the box.
Vervollständige die Fragen mit den Wörtern aus dem Kasten.

Have · have · Has · has · Has

1 What ______ you got in your pencil case?

2 ______ you got a ruler?

3 ______ your teacher got an English book?

4 What ______ your friend got in his schoolbag?

5 ______ she got a blue pen?

No, they haven't

3

Read the answers first. Then write the questions. **Lies zuerst die Antworten. Schreibe dann die Fragen.**

1 ______ No, I haven't got a new phone.

2 ______ No, we haven't got a rabbit cage.

3 ______ No, she hasn't got a skateboard.

Hi Ben!

4

Tim is helping Karla to write to Ben from Leeds. Write down her questions in English.
Tim hilft Karla, Ben aus Leeds zu schreiben. Schreibe ihre Fragen auf Englisch.

Beispiel: Karla: Wie frage ich, ob Ben Schwestern hat? Tim: *Have you got sisters?*

1 Karla: Wie frage ich, ob Ben Brüder hat?

Tim: ______

2 Karla: Wie frage ich, ob Ben einen Hund hat?

Tim: ______

3 Karla: Wie frage ich, ob Bens Hund ein Spielzeug hat?

Tim: ______

4 Karla: Wie frage ich, ob Ben eine Gitarre hat?

Tim: ______

5 Karla: Wie frage ich, ob Bens Mutter ein Skateboard hat?

Tim: ______

Over to you

Your class has new email partners in a school in England. How do you ask your new email partner what they have or haven't got? Deine Klasse hat neue E-Mail-Freunde in einer Schule in England. Wie fragst du einen neuen Freund / eine neue Freundin, was er oder sie hat oder nicht hat?

______

______

______

______

______

______

Introduction

Sit down and open your book, please.

Don't be late again, please.

Please open the window.

Don't forget your homework tomorrow.

Don't talk, please.

Listen to me, please.

Grammar Help

Mit der Befehlsform (Imperativ) bittest du jemanden, etwas zu tun.
Du stellst das Verb an den Satzanfang.
Pack your schoolbag.
Listen to the teacher.

Es ist höflicher, wenn du das Wort ***please*** hinzufügst:
Please close your book.
Don't close your book, ***please***.

Wenn du möchtest, dass jemand etwas nicht tut, stellst du ***don't*** vor das Verb.
Don't open the window.
Don't forget your homework.

Language Detective

a

Underline the imperative forms in the introduction text. Circle the forms in red that express that someone shouldn't do something. Unterstreiche die Befehlsformen im *Introduction*-Text. Kreise die Formen rot ein, die ausdrücken, dass jemand etwas nicht tun soll.

b

Fill in the table. Fülle die Tabelle aus.

Was die Schülerinnen und Schüler tun sollen	Was die Schülerinnen und Schüler nicht tun sollen
sit down and open their book	

In the classroom

1

Tick ✓ the sentences with an imperative form. **Setze ein Häkchen an die Sätze mit Imperativform.**

1 Tom opens the window. ☐
2 Please talk to a partner. ☐
3 Don't eat in the classroom, please. ☐
4 Sarah goes to the toilet. ☐
5 Eat in the cafeteria, please. ☐
6 Don't go to the toilet now! ☐
7 Open the window, please. ☐
8 Don't talk in class! ☐
9 We talk to our classmates. ☐
10 The teacher talks to a student. ☐
11 Don't open the window in winter. ☐
12 We always eat at lunchtime. ☐

At school

2

Which photo goes with which sentence? Write the letters in the table.
Welches Foto gehört zu welchem Satz? Schreibe die Buchstaben in die Tabelle.

A

B

C

D

E

F

G

H

1 Don't forget your exercise book.
2 Open your book, please.
3 Be on time.
4 Listen to me!
5 Sit down, please.
6 Work with a partner.
7 Don't run in the classroom.
8 Please sing along.

1	B
2	
3	
4	
5	
6	
7	
8	

What the teacher says

3

Complete the sentences with the right form of the imperative.
Vervollständige die Sätze mit der richtigen Imperativform.

1 *Don't go* ______ (not go) home now!

2 ______ (look at) the photos, please.

3 ______ (spell) the word "laboratory", please.

4 ______ (not talk to) your classmates, please!

5 ______ (not forget) your pencil case at home, please.

6 Please ______ (not use) your smartphone in class.

7 Always ______ (listen to) your teachers, please!

Say it in English

4

Write down the sentences in English. Schreibe die Sätze auf Englisch auf.

1 Mache dir keine Sorgen! ______

2 Packe bitte deine Schultasche. ______

3 Überprüfe dein Federmäppchen. ______

4 Vergiss bitte deine Schere nicht. ______

5 Sei nicht nervös. ______

Over to you

Write rules for your teachers. What should they do? What should they not do?
Schreibe Regeln für deine Lehrkräfte. Was sollen sie tun? Was sollen sie nicht tun?

______

______

______

______

Introduction

My schoolbag

This is my schoolbag. The schoolbag is open.
In my schoolbag there is a pencil case and there is a folder.
The pencil case is blue and the folder is green. There is an exercise book for my homework. It is an orange exercise book. There are three books: an English book, a maths book and a history book.
The English book is black. There is also a ruler in my schoolbag.
The ruler is yellow. The pencil case is also open. There are many pens and pencils, a pair of scissors and an eraser. There is no calculator.

Grammar Help

Auch im Englischen gibt es bestimmte Artikel (*definite articles*) und unbestimmte Artikel (*indefinite articles*). Es gibt nur eine Form des bestimmten Artikels, auch in der Mehrzahl: ***the***.
Für den unbestimmten Artikel benutzt du ***a*** oder ***an*** – je nachdem, ob das folgende Wort mit einem Vokallaut ausgesprochen wird oder nicht.

bestimmter Artikel	**unbestimmter Artikel (vor einem Konsonantenlaut)**	**unbestimmter Artikel (vor einem Vokallaut)**
the desk – der Schreibtisch **the** school – die Schule **the** books – die Bücher	**a** desk – ein Schreibtisch **a** school – eine Schule **a** uniform – eine Uniform (Aussprache: /ˈjunifoːm/)	**an** apple – ein Apfel **an** orange – eine Orange

Language Detective

a

Underline all the forms of the indefinite article in the introduction text in green and all the forms of the definite article in blue. Unterstreiche alle Formen des unbestimmten Artikels im Einführungstext grün und alle Formen des bestimmten Artikels blau.

b

Sort the nouns and write them down. Sortiere die Hauptwörter und schreibe sie auf.

the: ____________________

a: ____________________

an: ____________________

On the desk

1

Circle the right form. Kreise die richtige Form ein.

1 This is **an / a** pencil case.

2 In it, there is **the / they** red folder.

3 There is **an / a** eraser.

4 **There / The** eraser is green.

5 There is **an / a** calculator.

6 **The / They** calculator is black.

7 There is **an / a** pen.

8 It is **an / a** orange pen.

At school

2

Unscramble the sentences and write them down.
Bringe die Sätze in die richtige Reihenfolge und schreibe sie auf.

1 schoolbag – pencil case – is in – The – the – . ____________________

2 glue – desk – on – is – the – The – . ____________________

3 old English book – new English book. – I have got – and – a – an ____________________

____

4 new – black – is – English book – The – . ____________________

5 have got – apple – I – in my schoolbag – an – . ____________________

6 on – wall – There is – orange clock – the – an – . ____________________

Sue's school things

3

Fill in the articles: *the*, *a* or *an*. Trage die Artikel ein: *the*, *a* oder *an*.

Sue takes lots of things to school with her. In her schoolbag she has got ______ pencil case with ______ pen, ______ pencil, ______ ruler and ______ eraser. She has ______ English folder and ______ folder for maths. ______ English folder is red and ______ maths folder is blue. She also has ______ calculator. She needs ______ calculator for maths. In her lunchbox she has ______ sandwich and ______ orange. ______ sandwich has butter on it. After lunch she has PE. They play hockey on ______ sports field.

What's the word?

4

Circle the noun that goes with *an*. **Kreise das Hauptwort ein, das zu *an* gehört.**

1 eraser / book / pencil

2 folder / exercise book / ruler

3 pen / smartphone / orange

4 computer / bin / apple

5 calendar / poster / English book

6 animal / calculator / uniform

In the classroom

5

How do you say that in English? Write down the sentences.
Wie sagt man das auf Englisch? Schreibe die Sätze auf.

1 Wie sage ich, dass dort ein Computer und ein Kalender ist?

There is ______

2 Wie sage ich, dass dort ein Englischbuch ist?

______

3 Wie sage ich, dass dort ein Fenster und ein oranges Poster ist?

______

4 Wie sage ich, dass dort ein Lineal, ein Stift und ein Radiergummi ist?

______

5 Wie sage ich, dass dort ein Heft und ein Federmäppchen ist?

______

Over to you

Write down what you put in your schoolbag for the next day.
Schreibe auf, was du für den nächsten Tag in deine Schultasche packst.

______

______

______

Introduction

Hello everyone!
My name is Jack. Let me tell you about my classroom.

There are 18 children in my class, so we have ten desks and 18 chairs. There are 18 schoolbags and 18 pencil cases. There are lots of exercise books, pens, pencils and folders on the desks.
Every student has got a box with personal things in the classroom. The boxes are on the bookshelves. There are also lots of books on the bookshelves: school books and books with different stories. We also have some posters and photos.

Grammar Help

Wenn du über mehrere Dinge oder Personen sprechen willst, verwendest du die **Pluralformen der Nomen**. Man hängt an das Hauptwort ein **-s**. Es gibt aber auch unregelmäßige Pluralformen.

Singular	Plural
one book	two book**s**
one sandwi**ch**	two sandwi**ches**
one shel**f**	two shel**ves**
one stor**y**	two stor**ies**

!
Bei Nomen, die auf **-s**, **-ss**, **-sh**, **-ch** oder **-x** enden, hängst du im Plural ein **-es** an das Hauptwort an: *one box – two box**es***.
Endet ein Nomen im Singular auf **-f** oder **-fe**, hängst du im Plural ein **-ves** an: *one knife – two kni**ves***.
Bei Nomen, die auf **-y** enden und direkt davor einen Konsonanten haben, wird das -y im Plural zu **-ies**: *one story – two stor**ies***.
Es gibt ein paar Wörter, die keiner dieser Regeln folgen und die du beim Vokabellernen mitlernen musst: *one foot – two **feet**, one child – two **children***

Language Detective

a

Underline all the plural forms of the nouns in the introduction text. Use different colours: blue for regular forms and green for irregular forms.
Unterstreiche alle Pluralformen der Nomen im Einführungstext. Verwende unterschiedliche Farben: Blau für regelmäßige Formen und Grün für unregelmäßige Formen.

b

Write down the plural forms together with their singular forms.
Schreibe die Pluralformen zusammen mit ihren Singularformen auf.

children – child,

Reading is fun

1

Circle the right form. **Kreise die richtige Form ein.**

1 There are lots of **books / bookes** in my room.

2 They are on my **bookshelfs / bookshelves**.

3 There are three **childs / children** in the room.

4 Their **lifes / lives** are interesting.

5 They have all sorts of **hobbies / hobbys**.

6 Their **familys / families** are big.

7 The **cities / citys** they live in are famous.

8 Their **friendes / friends** are really nice.

In the photos

2

Write down what you see in the photos. **Schreibe auf, was du auf den Fotos siehst.**

1

There are two ______

2

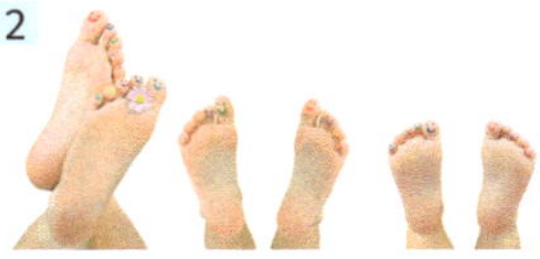

______

3

______

4

______

5

______

6

______

At school

3

Fill in the correct plural forms. **Trage die richtigen Pluralformen ein.**

I love my ______ (teacher). They always tell us funny ______ (story) of ______ (experiment) at the science club. One experiment is a trick: you take three ______ (lunchbox) and three ______ (sandwich). The ______ (child) close their ______ (eye). They touch their ______ (nose) and sing two ______ (song). They open their ______ (eye) again. There are no ______ (sandwich) in two of the ______ (lunchbox). Where are they?

Odd one out

4

Circle the odd one out. **Kreise das Wort ein, das nicht zu den anderen gehört.**

Achte auf die Pluralform, nicht auf die Wortbedeutung. !

1 assemblies / activities / actions
2 books / children / pens
3 boxes / sandwiches / posters
4 dads / cities / days
5 footballs / felt-tips / feet
6 friends / lives / bookshelves

Classroom talk

5

How do you say that in English? Write down the sentences.
Wie sagt man das auf Englisch? Schreibe die Sätze auf.

1 Wie sage ich, dass es in meiner Nachbarschaft viele Kinder gibt?

There are ______________________________

2 Wie sage ich, dass wir nachmittags viele Aktivitäten machen?

____

3 Wie sage ich, dass ich viele Hobbys habe?

____

4 Wie frage ich, ob ich die Fenster öffnen kann?

____

5 Wie frage ich, was in den Kisten auf den Bücherregalen ist?

____

Over to you

Describe your classroom. **Beschreibe dein Klassenzimmer.**

____

____

____

____

Introduction

Hi, I am Lisa. This is my school day:
Every day I go to school at 7:30am. I always take the bus.
At school I have lots of lessons. My favourite subject is music.
I like the music teacher.
At lunchtime I go to the school cafeteria. My friend Kate never goes there.
She always eats sandwiches from home.
On Wednesdays I go to the book club. At the book club we read a lot of books.
My friend Amy loves books, too. She always reads in the breaks.
Every Friday afternoon I go swimming with my class. I don't like swimming.
Every day I go home from school at 4pm.
I do my homework and then I watch TV. I go to bed at 9pm.
On Saturdays I go to bed at 11pm.

Grammar Help

DIGITAL+ video 30

Das ***simple present*** verwendest du, wenn jemand etwas **regelmäßig** tut oder etwas regelmäßig stattfindet. Du verwendest es auch, wenn etwas über längere Zeit stattfindet oder **allgemeingültig** ist.

Das ***simple present*** hat die gleiche Form wie die Grundform des Verbs.
Nur in der 3. Person (*he, she, it*) hängst du ein **-s** an:
I **get up** at 7:30. He **reads** many books.
Verneinungen bildest du mit ***don't*** oder ***doesn't***:
I **don't** like chocolate. She **doesn't** eat much.

! Bei ***do*** und ***go*** und wenn das Verb auf **-ss**, **-sh**, **-ch** oder **-x** endet, hängst du ein **-es** in der 3. Person Singular an:
Sam ***watches*** *a film.* / *She often* ***goes*** *to the cinema.*
Endet das Verb auf **-y** und steht ein Konsonant davor, wird es zu **-ies**:
Mel ***worries*** *about her first day.*
(Aber: *Mel plays football.*)

Language Detective

a

Underline all the simple present forms in the introduction text.
Unterstreiche alle Formen der einfachen Gegenwart im Einführungstext.

b

Sort the simple present forms into the table.
Sortiere die Formen der einfachen Gegenwart in die Tabelle ein.

I/we	*am, go,*
he/she/it	*is,*

Thursday afternoons

1

Unscramble the sentences and write them down.
Bringe die Sätze in die richtige Reihenfolge und schreibe sie auf.

1 Thursday – uncle – Every – my – I see – . ______

2 like – very much – him – I – . ______

3 He – in the – me – park – meets – . ______

4 basketball – play – together – We – football and – . ______

5 a lot of – We – songs – together – sing – . ______

6 buys – an – always – ice cream – me – He – . ______

7 sometimes – We – board games – play – . ______

What is right?

2

Circle the right form. **Kreise die richtige Form ein.**

1 He **touchs / touches** his nose.

2 She **dos / does** her homework.

3 She **watches / watchs** a film.

4 He **meetes / meets** his friends.

5 She **haves / has** a question.

6 She **teachs / teaches** history.

7 He **goes / gos** to school.

8 She **says / sayes** her name.

Odd one out

3

Circle the odd one out. **Kreise das Wort ein, das nicht zu den anderen gehört.**

Achte auf die Wortendung, nicht auf die Wortbedeutung. !

1 tries / buys / worries

2 starts / misses / collects

3 writes / lives / copies

4 teaches / tells / finds

5 matches / chooses / completes

6 goes / says / sees

7 plays / worries / buys

8 does / reads / draws

My brother's school

4

Complete the sentences with the right forms of the simple present.
Vervollständige die Sätze mit den richtigen Formen der einfachen Gegenwart.

My brother ______________ (walk) to school every day. He ______________ (meet) his friends at the park and they ______________ (walk) together. They ______________ (wear) a cool school uniform: a black pair of trousers and a white shirt. My brother really ______________ (hate) it, but I ______________ (like) it very much. I ______________ (think) it is cool. And they ______________ (have) interesting school clubs: a science club and a music club. His teacher ______________ (do) a lot of experiments at the science club and ______________ (play) the guitar at the music club. He ______________ (have) a cool red guitar and they ______________ (sing) a lot of songs together. I also ______________ (want) to go to my brother's school, but I ______________ (go) to another school. We ______________ (have) no school uniforms and no school clubs.

I don't like Mondays

5

Complete the sentences with *don't* or *doesn't*.
Vervollständige die Sätze mit *don't* oder *doesn't*.

I ______________ like Mondays. I ______________ have my favourite subjects on Mondays and I ______________ see my friends Sue and Helen. They ______________ go to the music or to the book club with me on Mondays. Helen ______________ like music and ______________ go to the music club and Sue ______________ like books and ______________ go to the book club. And after school they ______________ have time for me. They go to football training and I ______________ like football and ______________ go there. And we get a lot of homework on Mondays. I ______________ want to do homework. I really ______________ like Mondays!

Different school clubs

6

How do you say that in English? Write down the sentences.
Wie sagt man das auf Englisch? Schreibe die Sätze auf.

1 Wie sage ich, dass die Buch-AG interessant klingt?

2 Wie sage ich, dass meine Schwester Teamsportarten nicht mag?

3 Wie sage ich, dass mein Bruder montags immer in die Cafeteria geht?

4 Wie sage ich, dass die Naturwissenschafts-AG nicht schlecht klingt?

5 Wie sage ich, dass der Musiklehrer manchmal Gitarre spielt?

Over to you

Write down what you do at school every day of the week.
Schreibe auf, was du jeden Tag der Woche in der Schule machst.

Introduction

Hello Tilda!

I want to make a presentation about German schools and have a lot of questions.
When does your school start? Do you go to school every day? Who are your friends? What are your favourite subjects? How do you get to school? Do you walk? Does your mum take you to school? Do you have school clubs in the afternoon? Do you like your school?

Thanks for your answers, Bob

Grammar Help

DIGITAL+ video 30

Es gibt zwei Arten von Fragen: **Entscheidungsfragen** und **Fragen mit Fragewort**.
Auf Entscheidungsfragen kann man nur mit „ja“ oder „nein“ antworten. Im Englischen wiederholt man dabei in einer Kurzantwort die passende Form der einfachen Gegenwart aus der jeweiligen Frage:
Can you swim? – Yes, I can. *Are you Sarah? – No, I'm not.*
In Fragen ohne *can* oder *be* stellst du ***do*** oder ***does*** an den Satzanfang:
***Do** you **live** in London?– Yes, I **do**. / No, I **don't**.*
***Does** she **like** bananas?– Yes, she **does**. / No, she **doesn't**.*

Bei Fragen mit Fragewort steht das Fragewort am Satzanfang, vor ***do*** oder ***does***:
***What do** you **think** of rock music?*
***When does** the book club **meet**?*
Ausnahme: Wenn *who* nach dem Subjekt fragt, brauchst du kein zusätzliches *do* oder *does*:
***Who lives** in London? Nina lives in London*

Language Detective

a

Underline *do* and *does* in the introduction text. Circle all the question words.
Unterstreiche *do* und *does* im Einführungstext. Kreise alle Fragewörter ein.

b

Write down one question with a question word and one question that starts with *do* or *does*. Explain the difference in German. Schreibe eine Frage mit Fragewort auf und eine Frage mit *do* oder *does*. Erkläre den Unterschied auf Deutsch.

What's on?

1

Circle the right form. Kreise die richtige Form ein.

1 **Do / Does** you go to the school band?
2 **Do / Does** Helen go to the cooking club?
3 **Where / What** does the book club meet?
4 **When / What** do they do at the science club?
5 **Who / Where** practises at the gym?
6 **Do / Does** we meet in the music room?
7 **What / When** does the drama club meet?
8 **Do / Does** the teacher do experiments?

At the new school

2

Unscramble the questions and write them down.
Bringe die Fragen in die richtige Reihenfolge und schreibe sie auf.

1 your – do you – new school – How – like – ? __________
2 like best – What – do you – subjects – ? __________
3 is – teacher – favourite – Who – your – ? __________
4 go to – Do – drama club – the – you – ? __________
5 Where – drama club – the – meet – does – ? __________
6 practise – rains – you – do – when – Where – it – football – ? __________

Good to know

3

Make questions with *do* or *does*. Bilde Fragen mit *do* oder *does*.

1 you / go to / the football team / after school *Do you go to the football team after school?*
2 Ella / play the guitar / in the school band __________
3 we / have / homework __________
4 you / wear / a school uniform __________
5 your friend / go to / your school __________
6 your school uniform / look nice __________

About school

4

Complete the sentences with the right question words from the box.
Vervollständige die Sätze mit den richtigen Fragewörtern aus dem Kasten.

Where · Who · How · When · What · When · Where · What

1 ______ do you go to school? – I go to school at 7:45am.

2 ______ is your favourite classmate? – Amy is my favourite classmate.

3 ______ is the school library? – The school library is next to the science lab.

4 ______ is your favourite subject? – History is my favourite subject.

5 ______ is your first break? – Our first break is at 10:30am.

6 ______ does the school band practise? – The school band practises in the music room.

7 ______ does your mum think about the science club? – She thinks it's interesting.

8 ______ do you like maths? – I think maths is OK.

What's the question?

5

Make questions for the underlined elements of the sentences.
Bilde Fragen zu den unterstrichenen Elementen der Sätze.

1 Ben goes to school at 8:00am. *When does Ben go to school?*

2 The book club meets in the library. ______

3 The science club does experiments. ______

4 Maria always plays football on Mondays. ______

5 Joe likes vanilla ice cream. ______

6 Yes, we have a lot of books. ______

7 No, Susie doesn't like chocolate cake. ______

At school

6

How do you say that in English? Write down the questions.
Wie sagt man das auf Englisch? Schreibe die Fragen auf.

1 Wie frage ich, ob wir Hausaufgaben haben?

2 Wie frage ich, wo die Bibliothek ist?

3 Wie frage ich, ob jemand Pizza mag?

4 Wie frage ich, wann sich die Schulband trifft?

5 Wie frage ich, wer die Musiklehrerin ist?

Over to you

You write to your new pen friend in England. Ask him or her all you want to know about his or her school clubs. Write down your questions.
Du schreibst deinem neuen Brieffreund / deiner neuen Brieffreundin in England. Frage ihn oder sie alles, was du über seine oder ihre Schul-AGs wissen möchtest. Schreibe deine Fragen auf.

Introduction

Saturdays are great! Our family eats breakfast in the kitchen.

We have a lot of time. We drink tea and milk, and we eat toast, butter, tomatoes, bacon and eggs.

Then we play football in the park and my parents take the dog for a long walk.

We cook a nice family dinner in the evening. Then we watch TV or play board games.

Grammar Help

Aussagesätze werden im Englischen nach einem bestimmten Muster gebildet.
Subjekt, Verb und Objekt stehen immer in dieser Reihenfolge: **S**ubjekt – **V**erb – **O**bjekt (**S – V – O**)
Im Anschluss können noch weitere Ergänzungen folgen.

Subjekt	Verb	Objekt	Ergänzung
Sue	plays	football.	
Thilo	meets	the children	in the park.

Anstatt ein Nomen mehrmals zu verwenden, kannst du es durch ein Personalpronomen ersetzen, wenn klar ist, worauf es sich bezieht: **Thilo** meets **the children** in the park. ⇨ **He** meets **them** in the park.

Stehen die Personalpronomen *I, you, he, she, it, we* und *they* in der Objektposition, verwendest du die Objektpronomen *me, you, him, her, it, us* und *them*.

Language Detective

a

Underline all the subjects in the introduction text in green, all the verbs in red and all the objects in blue.

Unterstreiche im Einführungstext alle Subjekte in Grün, alle Verben in Rot und alle Objekte in Blau.

b

Write down three sentences from the introduction text in the table.

Schreibe drei Sätze aus dem Einführungstext in die Tabelle.

Subjekt	Verb	Objekt (mit Ergänzung)

My family

1

Circle the right sentence. Kreise den richtigen Satz ein.

1 I am in the bathroom at 10:00. / I am at 10:00 in the bathroom.

2 We clean every Saturday our ears. / We clean our ears every Saturday.

3 My little sister in the morning goes to school. / My little sister goes to school in the morning.

4 My big brother brushes his teeth every evening. / My big brother every evening brushes his teeth.

5 My mum plays hockey every Wednesday. / My mum every Wednesday plays hockey.

I love toast

2

Unscramble the sentences and write them down.
Bringe die Sätze in die richtige Reihenfolge und schreibe sie auf.

1 love – toast and butter – in the morning – I – . ______

2 in the evening – Our family – TV – watches – . ______

3 our grandparents – visit – every Sunday – We – . ______

4 at the weekend – My brother – tennis – plays – . ______

5 My sister – pictures – in the afternoon – draws – . ______

6 play – and dad – board games – with us – My mum – . ______

She meets him at the weekend

3

Write the sentences with the personal pronouns. **Schreibe die Sätze mit den Personalpronomen.**

1 **Fiona** meets **Felix** at the weekend. *She meets him at the weekend.*

2 **The children** see **their teachers** at school. ______

3 **Max** likes **Somaya** a lot. ______

4 **Lily and I** want to see **you and Tom** tomorrow. ______

5 **The cake** is delicious. **Lucy** really likes **the cake.** ______

Odd one out

4

Circle the odd one out. **Kreise den Ausdruck ein, der nicht zu den anderen passt.**

1 in the park / in the morning / in the house

2 in the morning / at school / in the afternoon

3 at the café / at the weekend / at the restaurant

4 on Saturday / on the table / on Sunday

5 in the evening / in the living room / in the bedroom

6 in the house / in the garden / in the afternoon

Say it in English

5

How do you say that in English? Write down the sentences.
Wie sagt man das auf Englisch? Schreibe die Sätze auf.

1 Wie sage ich, dass ich nachmittags meine Hausaufgaben mache?

I do

2 Wie sage ich, dass ich meine Freunde auf dem Spielplatz treffe?

3 Wie sage ich, dass mein Vater sonntags Basketball spielt?

4 Wie sage ich, dass meine Mutter abends liest?

5 Wie sage ich, dass unser Hund nachmittags im Park spielt?

Over to you

Write down what you eat for breakfast on Saturdays and what you do.
Schreibe auf, was du samstags zum Frühstück isst und was du machst.

Introduction

Hello Lisa!
My name is Kharim. Today I want to tell you about the afternoon activities at my school.
We have a music club where we can sing and play the guitar, but we can't play the piano.
We can also swim or play football and hockey, but we can't play basketball or volleyball.
Then we can play table tennis, but we can't play tennis.
But the best is that we can ride horses at my school.
I love it!
Please write back soon. Kharim

Grammar Help

DIGITAL+ video 31

Wenn du sagen möchtest, was jemand tun kann oder darf, benutzt du ***can***.
Can steht mit der Grundform des Verbs und bleibt in allen Personen gleich.

I **can** swim. She **can** dance. We **can** play the guitar. Mum says I **can** go to the party.

Mit ***can't*** (bzw. seltener: ***cannot***) kann man ausdrücken, dass etwas nicht erlaubt ist oder dass man etwas nicht tun kann:
You **can't** swim here. I **can't** speak French.

Language Detective

Tick ✓ the things that Kharim can do at his school and put a cross X in the box next to the things that he can't do.
Mache ein Häkchen bei den Dingen, die Kharim an seiner Schule machen kann, und setze ein Kreuz in die Kästchen neben den Dingen, die er nicht tun kann.

1 They can play the piano. ☐
2 They can play the guitar. ☐
3 They can play tennis. ☐
4 They can play table tennis. ☐
5 They can play basketball. ☐
6 They can play hockey and football. ☐
7 They can sing. ☐
8 They can swim. ☐
9 They can ride horses. ☐
10 They can play volleyball. ☐

What you can and can't do

1

Which picture goes with which sentence? Write the letters in the table.
Welches Bild gehört zu welchem Satz? Schreibe die Buchstaben in die Tabelle.

A

B

C

D

E

F

G

H

1 The boy can play the guitar.
2 You can't swim here.
3 The girl can play hockey.
4 You can't walk your dog here.
5 You can't run here.
6 The boy can play basketball.
7 The girl can play the piano.
8 You can't ride your bike here.

1	B
2	
3	
4	
5	
6	
7	
8	

Different activities

2

Complete the sentences with *can* or *can't*. Vervollständige die Sätze *can* oder *can't*.

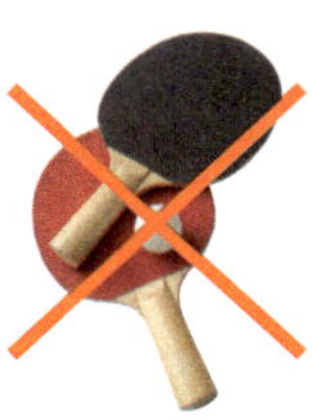

1 Tia ______________ play the guitar.
2 Tia ______________ ride a bike.
3 Tia ______________ play computer games.
4 Tia ______________ play table tennis.
5 Tia ______________ do karate.

At the break

3

Write down what students can do during the break.
Schreibe auf, was Schülerinnen und Schüler in der Pause tun können.

play · listen to music · eat · drink · ...

Say it in English

4

How do you say that in English? Write down the sentences.
Wie sagt man das auf Englisch? Schreibe die Sätze auf.

1 Wie sage ich, dass ich Englisch sprechen kann?

I can

2 Wie sage ich, dass wir im Park Fußball spielen können?

3 Wie sage ich, dass mein Hund nicht klettern kann?

4 Wie sage ich, dass meine kleine Schwester Fahrrad fahren kann?

Over to you

You write an email to your partner school in England. Write about what you can or can't do at your school in the afternoon.
Du schreibst deiner Partnerschule in England eine E-Mail. Schreibe darüber, was man an eurer Schule am Nachmittag machen oder nicht machen kann.

At my school we can

Introduction

Hello Kharim!
Thanks for your email about your school activities.
Can you also play other instruments at the music club?
Where can you play instruments at school?
And what about different sports? Can you do karate or judo at your school? Can you climb or do athletics?
Where can you do that? At the gym? When can you do the sports?
And what about other activities? Can you do arts and crafts? I love arts and crafts!
Please write back soon. Lisa

Grammar Help

DIGITAL+ video 31

Wenn du fragen möchtest, was jemand tun oder nicht tun kann, benutzt du ***can*** bzw. ***can't***.
Mit ***can*** bzw. ***can't*** kannst du auch danach fragen, was erlaubt oder nicht erlaubt ist.

Frage	Antwort
Can I swim?	Yes, you **can**. / No, you **can't**.
Can we go to the party?	Yes, you **can**. / No, you **can't**.

Bei Fragen mit Fragewort stellst du das Fragewort an den Satzanfang, noch vor can.

Frage	Kurzantwort
Where can you play football?	In the park.
When can I go to the park?	In the afternoon.

Language Detective

a

Underline all the verb forms with *can* and all the questions words in the introduction text.
Use different colours: green for all the verb forms with *can* and blue for all the question words.
Unterstreiche alle Verbformen mit *can* und alle Fragewörter im Einführungstext.
Verwende unterschiedliche Farben: Grün für alle Verbformen mit *can* und Blau für alle Fragewörter.

b

Circle the correct questions. Kreise die richtigen Fragen ein.

1 Where you can play instruments? / Where can you play instruments?

2 Can you do athletics? / Can do you athletics?

3 When can you do the sports? / When you can do the sports?

4 Do you can arts and crafts? / Can you do arts and crafts?

Many questions

1

Unscramble the questions and write them down.
Bringe die Fragen in die richtige Reihenfolge und schreibe sie auf.

1 you – speak – Can – English – ? ____________

2 Can – to school – by bike – go – you – ? ____________

3 do – your dad – athletics – Can – ? ____________

4 Can – tricks – skateboard – do – your cat – ? ____________

5 mum – dance – your – Can – ? ____________

6 now – brother – Can – the cinema – go to – your – ? ____________

More questions

2

Complete the questions with the words from the box. Then write answers.
Vervollständige die Fragen mit den Wörtern aus dem Kasten. Schreibe dann Antworten.

Where · What · Who · When · What

1 ____________ can you do in the afternoon? ____________

2 ____________ can you go after school? ____________

3 ____________ can you do at the weekend? ____________

4 ____________ can you take the dog for a walk in the park? ____________

5 ____________ can do the shopping today? ____________

No, they haven't

3

Read the answers first. Then write the questions. **Lies zuerst die Antworten. Schreibe dann die Fragen.**

1 ____________ No, I can't do karate.

2 ____________ No, we can't listen to music now.

3 ____________ Yes, I can dance.

Say it in English

4

How do you say that in English? Write down the questions.

Wie sagt man das auf Englisch? Schreibe die Fragen auf.

1 Wie frage ich, ob du Englisch sprechen kannst?

Can ______

2 Wie frage ich, ob ich auf den Spielplatz gehen darf?

______

3 Wie frage ich, wann ich Gitarre spielen darf?

______

4 Wie frage ich, ob ich Fernsehen gucken darf?

______

5 Wie frage ich, wo ich mich hinsetzen darf?

______

6 Wie frage ich, was du am Nachmittag tun kannst?

______

7 Wie frage ich, ob ich etwas Milch trinken darf?

______

Over to you

You want to know what the students can or can't do in the afternoon at your partner school in England. Ask questions.

Du möchtest wissen, was die Schülerinnen und Schüler an deiner Partnerschule in England am Nachmittag machen können. Stelle Fragen.

______

______

______

______

Introduction

Grammar Help

What, ***where***, ***when*** und ***who*** sind Fragewörter.
Wenn du eine Frage mit einem Fragewort stellen möchtest, stellst du das Fragewort an den Satzanfang.

what	where	when	who
What do you think? **What** can I do? **What** have I got? **What** is the problem?	**Where** can you go? **Where** do they play?	**When** have they got maths? **When** is your birthday? **When** do you go to school?	**Who** do you see in the photo? **Who** can we meet?

Achtung! Fragen mit ***who*** brauchen kein zusätzliches ***do*** oder ***does***, wenn du nach dem Subjekt fragst:
Who goes to school? (**Wer** geht in die Schule?) **Who** can we meet? (**Wen** können wir treffen?)

Language Detective

a

Look at the questions in the introduction text. Underline all the verb forms. Use different colours: red for questions with *do/does*, blue for questions with *can*, green for questions with *have got* und black for questions with *be*.

Sieh dir die Fragen im Einführungstext an. Unterstreiche alle Verbformen. Verwende unterschiedliche Farben: Rot für Fragen mit *do/does*, Blau für Fragen mit *can*, Grün für Fragen mit *have got* und Schwarz für Fragen mit *be*.

b

Compare the questions with *have got* and *be* to the questions with *do/does* and *can*. What do you notice? Tick. ✓

Vergleiche die Fragen mit *have got* und *be* mit den Fragen mit *do/does* und *can*. Was fällt dir auf? Mache ein Häkchen.

- ☐ Das Fragewort steht an einer anderen Stelle.
- ☐ Ich sehe keinen Unterschied.
- ☐ Es gibt bei den Fragen mit *do/does* und *can* immer noch eine weitere Verbform im Satz.

At home

1

Unscramble the questions and write them down.
Bringe die Fragen in die richtige Reihenfolge und schreibe sie auf.

1 the breakfast table – do you – come to – When – ? ______

2 want to – What – do you – eat – ? ______

3 on – is – Who – the phone – ? ______

4 the butter – Where – find – I – can – ? ______

5 How – like – toast – your – you – do – ? ______

6 can – our – go to – rooms – When – we – ? ______

7 What – want to – in the afternoon – you – do – do – ? ______

8 you – do – meet – want to – Where – ? ______

At a new school

2

Fill in the correct forms of *do* or *does*. **Trage die richtigen Formen von *do* oder *does* ein.**

1 When ______ school start?

2 Where ______ we have to go for our lunch break?

3 Who ______ I sit next to?

4 What ______ our teacher say in the morning?

5 How ______ Ellie get to school?

6 How ______ I get to school?

7 When ______ we have lunch break?

8 Where ______ we go to for the book club?

A school day

3

Fill in the correct forms of *have got*. Trage die richtigen Formen von *have got* ein.

1 Where has she got ____ (she) her pencil case?

2 Where ____ (we) our English books?

3 Who ____ a ruler?

4 What ____ (you) in your schoolbag?

5 When ____ (he) his maths test?

6 Where ____ (we) got PE?

Afternoon activities

4

Fill in the correct forms of *be*. Trage die richtigen Formen von *be* ein.

1 Where ____ I today?

2 When ____ the sports club?

3 Who ____ in the sports club with me?

4 Where ____ my classmates today?

5 When ____ their clubs?

6 Where ____ my sports clothes?

What can we do?

5

Write questions with *can*. Schreibe Fragen mit *can*.

1 ____ ? (where / go swimming / I)

2 ____ ? (when / play with your friends / you)

3 ____ ? (what / drink for breakfast / he)

4 ____ ? (who / meet in the afternoon / we)

Classroom talk

6

How do you say that in English? Write down the questions.
Wie sagt man das auf Englisch? Schreibe die Fragen auf.

1 Wie frage ich, was ich für den Test brauche?

What do I

2 Wie frage ich, wie spät es ist?

3 Wie frage ich, was wir am Nachmittag machen?

4 Wie frage ich, wann ich zur Toilette gehen kann?

5 Wie frage ich, wer unser neuer Kunstlehrer ist?

6 Wie frage ich, wann die Mittagspause ist?

7 Wie frage ich, was wir nach der Pause machen wollen?

Over to you

Imagine you have a new email partner in a different country. What do you want to know? Ask questions and use question words. Stell dir vor, du hast einen neuen E-Mail-Partner / eine neue E-Mail-Partnerin in einem anderen Land. Was möchtest du wissen? Stelle Fragen und verwende Fragwörter.

Introduction

Hi, I'm Anna! This is a photo of my family. Our home is in Cardiff in Wales.

On the left you can see my uncle next to my grandmother and her new partner. Next to him there is my father with my younger sister Rosie. Our mother is not in the photo, but you can see Rosie's teddybear. She takes it everywhere.

On the right you can see my aunt. My aunt's dog is very cute. His name is Woof. Woof's favourite toys are balloons.

Grammar Help

Wenn du sagen möchtest, wem oder zu wem etwas gehört, kannst du dies mit dem s-Genitiv ausdrücken. Im Singular hängst du einen Apostroph und ein s an:
Karla**'s** room is tidy. Dennis**'s** cat is grey.

Das machst du auch bei unregelmäßigen Pluralformen, die nicht auf **-s** enden: The children**'s** room is big.

Bei regelmäßigen Pluralformen fügst du nur einen Apostroph an das Plural-s an:
The girls**'** room is big.

Man kann statt eines Nomens mit s-Genitiv auch Possessivbegleiter *(possessive forms)* verwenden:
Eve lives in a house. **Her** room is small.

Englische Possessivbegleiter sind:
my, your, his, her, its, our, your, their

Wenn etwas zu einer Sache gehört, verwendet man meist eine Konstruktion mit ***of***:
The name **of** the school is Holland Park School.

Language Detective

a

Underline the forms of the s-genitive and the possessive forms in the introduction text.
Unterstreiche die Formen des s-Genitivs und die Possessivbegleiter im Einführungstext.

b

Circle the right forms. **Kreise die richtigen Formen ein.**

1 My **dogs' / dog's** name is Woof.
2 **His / Him** favourite toys are balloons.
3 My **parents' / parent's** names are Doris and Eric.
4 **They / Their** house is small.
5 My **uncle's / uncles** name is Thomas.
6 Uncle **Thomas / Thomas's** car is old.
7 My **aunt's / aunts'** name is Lisa.
8 **She / Her** hobby is reading.

Word search

1

Find the possessive forms in the word search and write them down. → ↓
Finde die Formen der Possessivbegleiter im Wortsuchrätsel und schreibe sie auf. → ↓

O	M	N	T	E	Y	G	I
H	Y	E	R	T	O	E	T
A	U	R	H	M	U	D	H
O	U	R	H	I	R	T	E
I	Y	B	I	A	I	E	I
T	O	B	S	E	M	P	R
S	U	U	Y	M	Y	A	E
E	T	Z	H	E	R	R	T

our ____________

____

____

____

____

____

____

Sophie

2

Complete the sentences with possessive forms.
Vervollständige die Sätze mit Possessivbegleitern.

1 I'm Sophie. ____________ favourite teacher is ____________ maths teacher.

2 ____________ friend's name is Sevda. ____________ parents are really nice.

3 Who is ____________ favourite teacher?

4 ____________ brother's cat is grey. ____________ hamsters are white and black.

5 ____________ sisters are twins. ____________ names are Judy and Trudy.

Many words

3

Circle the possessive forms. **Kreise die Possessivbegleiter ein.**

1 I / my / he
2 his / he / she
3 she / we / her
4 you / your / we
5 us / me / our
6 me / I / my
7 it / its / it's
8 they / them / their

A family tree

4

Complete the sentences with forms of the s-genitive. **Vervollständige die Sätze mit s-Genitivformen.**

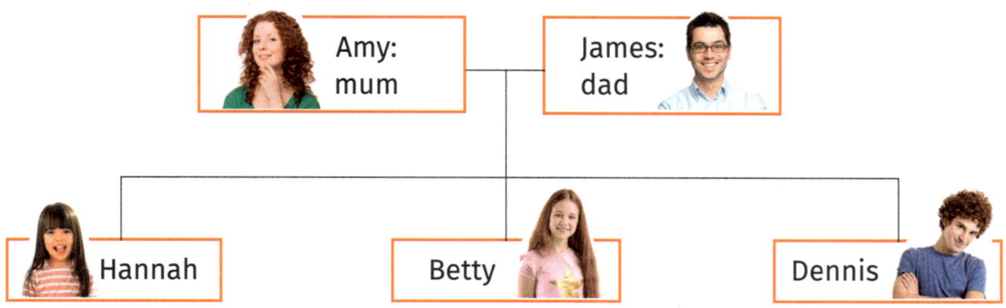

1 *Betty's* ________ mum is Amy.

2 ________ sisters are Hannah and Betty.

3 Hannah and ________ brother is Dennis.

4 Hannah, Betty and ________ dad is James.

5 Dennis and ________ sister is Betty.

6 *H* ________ dad is James.

7 *D* ________ mum is Amy.

8 *B* ________ dad is James.

Our house

5

Unscramble the sentences and write them down.
Bringe die Sätze in die richtige Reihenfolge und schreibe sie auf.

1 parents' – is – My – house – nice – . ________

2 My – is – room – small – brother's – . ________

3 two sisters' – big – is – My – room – . ________

4 cat's – is – toy – a yellow – Our – ball – . ________

5 is – four hamsters' – very big – cage – Our – . ________

6 dog – Thomas's – old – My brother – is – . ________

Say it in English

6

How do you say that in English? Write down the sentences.
Wie sagt man das auf Englisch? Schreibe die Sätze auf.

1 Wie sage ich, dass ich mein Zimmer gerne mag?

2 Wie sage ich, dass meine Brüder ihren Hund immer im Park ausführen?

3 Wie sage ich, dass Mary seine Schwester ist?

4 Wie sage ich, dass Herr Miller unser Lehrer ist?

5 Wie sage ich, dass meine Mutter ihrer Mutter jeden Freitag hilft?

Over to you

Choose three people you know. Write a short text about them. Use possessive forms and the s-genitive.
Wähle drei Menschen aus, die du kennst. Schreibe einen kurzen Text über sie. Verwende Possessivbegleiter und den s-Genitiv.

Introduction

My brother never does anything at home. I always help my parents with the chores at home. I always make my bed and tidy my room. My brother never makes his bed and he never tidies his room! My mum often does the shopping and the cooking and I sometimes help her. My dad often sets the table and cleans the kitchen. He usually takes out the rubbish. I am always there to help. I always empty the dishwasher. My brother is never at home. He never helps with the cooking. It's not fair!

Grammar Help

Die Wörter ***always***, ***usually***, ***often***, ***sometimes*** und ***never*** nennt man Häufigkeitsadverbien. Mit ihnen kannst du ausdrücken, wie häufig etwas geschieht.
Anders als im Deutschen stehen die Häufigkeitsadverbien fast immer vor dem Verb (Subjekt – Häufigkeitsadverb – Verb):
I **always** do my homework.
My mother **never** plays with our dog.

Nur in Sätzen mit ***be*** stehen die Häufigkeitsadverbien nach ***am***, ***are*** oder ***is***:
He **is usually** at home on Saturdays.
We **are often** at the playground on Sundays.

Language Detective

a

Underline the verbs in the introduction text in red and the adverbs of frequency in blue.
Unterstreiche die Verben im Einführungstext in Rot und alle Häufigkeitsadverbien in Blau.

b

Find two sentences with the word order *subject – adverb of frequency – verb* and two sentences with the word order *subject – verb – adverb of frequency*. Copy them.
Finde zwei Sätze, deren Satzstellung Subjekt – Häufigkeitsadverb – Verb ist und zwei Sätze, deren Satzstellung Subjekt – Verb – Häufigkeitsadverb ist. Schreibe sie ab.

1 ______

2 ______

3 ______

4 ______

Jobs at home

1

Make sentences. Bilde Sätze.

		do	
		does	
	always	set	the cooking.
I	usually	sets	the table.
Sophia	often	clean	the kitchen.
…	sometimes	cleans	the living room.
	never	vacuum	…
		vacuums	
		…	

Household chores

2

Circle the right form. Kreise die richtige Form ein.

1 I **always clean / clean always** my bedroom.

2 I **never am / am never** late.

3 I **play often / often play** football in the garden.

4 I **am always / always am** at home on Fridays.

5 You **usually go / go usually** to school.

Rob

3

Write sentences about Rob. Schreibe Sätze über Rob.

1 clean the bathroom (usually) *Rob usually cleans the bathroom.*

2 make the bed (sometimes)

3 vacuum the living room (never)

4 take out the rubbish (always)

Sharing the chores

4

How do you say that in English? Write down the sentences.
Wie sagt man das auf Englisch? Schreibe die Sätze auf.

1 Wie sage ich, dass meine Brüder unseren Eltern immer helfen?

2 Wie sage ich, dass meine Schwester normalerweise den Tisch deckt?

3 Wie sage ich, dass ich oft das Wohnzimmer staubsauge?

4 Wie sage ich, dass meine Mutter immer einkauft?

5 Wie sage ich, dass mein Vater manchmal kocht?

Over to you

Write down how you and your family share the chores at home. Use *always*, *usually*, *often*, *sometimes* and *never*.
Schreibe auf, wie du und deine Familie die Arbeiten zu Hause aufteilt. Verwende *immer*, *normalerweise*, *oft*, *manchmal* und *nie*.

Introduction

Hi, my name is Jackie and this is my friend Laura. We're sitting in my room at the moment and we're doing our homework. We are preparing a presentation about animals for our science class.
I am sitting in front of the computer and Laura is watching me – and she's taking notes. We are looking at a lot of interesting fact files and Laura is writing down some information.

Grammar Help

DIGITAL+ video 32

Mit der Verlaufsform der Gegenwart (***present progressive***) drückst du aus, was jemand gerade tut oder was gerade passiert. Die Handlungen sind noch nicht abgeschlossen.

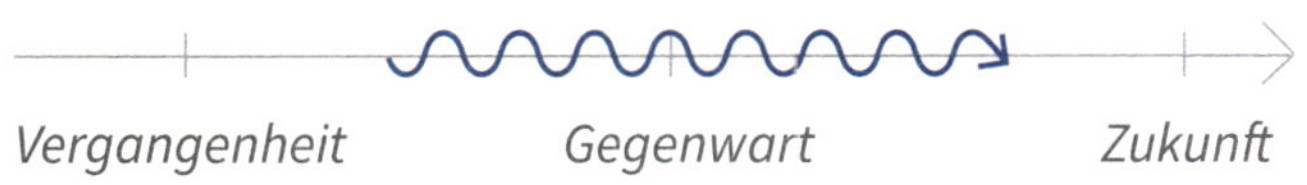

> **!** Endet das Verb auf -e, fällt das -e in der Verlaufsform weg: write → writing.
> Endet das Verb auf einem kurzen, betonten Vokal + Konsonant, wird der Konsonant verdoppelt: put → putting, run → running.

So bildest du das ***present progressive***:
Form von ***be*** (***am***, ***are***, ***is***) + **ing-Form des Verbs.**

Aussagesatz:	I **am** eat**ing** pizza.	They **are** talk**ing** to you.
Verneinung:	I **am not** eat**ing** pizza.	They **aren't** talk**ing** to you.

Language Detective

a

Underline the verbs in the present progressive form in the introduction text.
Unterstreiche die Verben im *present progressive* im Einführungstext.

b

How do you say that in English? Find the verb forms in the introduction text and write them down.
Wie sagt man das auf Englisch? Finde die Verbformen im Einführungstext und schreibe sie auf.

wir sitzen gerade	______	ich sitze gerade	______
wir machen gerade	______	sie macht gerade Notizen	______
wir bereiten gerade vor	______	sie schreibt gerade auf	______

At the moment

1

Circle the right verb form. **Kreise die richtge Verbform ein.**

1 I **am / is / are** talking to you.

2 Toby **am / is / are** doing his homework.

3 We **am / is / are** walking to school.

4 My parents **am / is / are** watching TV.

5 She **am / is / are** writing invitations.

6 They **am / is / are** baking a cake.

A Saturday at my place

2

Complete the sentences with *progressive forms.*
Vervollständige die Sätze mit dem *present progressive.*

This Saturday, my family is very busy. My dad *is cleaning* (clean) the bathroom. I ____________ (empty) the dishwasher and my sister ____________ (do) the shopping. My mum ____________ (tidy) the living room. My brother ____________ (vacuum) all the rooms. We ____________ (clean) the house together. In the afternoon we ____________ (go) to the park. We ____________ (take) the dog out for a walk. My brother ____________ (show) us some skateboard tricks. My sister ____________ (ride) her bike and I ____________ (play) with our dog. My parents ____________ (talk) about the week.

Different people

3

Write down what the people are doing or not doing.
Schreibe auf, was die Menschen gerade machen oder nicht machen.

1 

2 

3 

4 

1 *They are eating ice cream.*

2 ____________

3 ____________

4 ____________

Say it in English

4

How do you say that in English? Write down the sentences.
Wie sagt man das auf Englisch? Schreibe die Sätze auf.

1 Wie sage ich, dass mein Vater gerade die Spülmaschine ausräumt?

2 Wie sage ich, dass meine Schwester gerade aufräumt?

3 Wie sage ich, dass meine Mutter gerade staubsaugt?

4 Wie sage ich, dass mein Bruder gerade einkauft?

5 Wie sage ich, dass ich gerade koche?

Over to you

Write down what you and your family are doing at the moment. Use the *present progressive*.
Schreibe auf, was du und deine Familie im Moment machen. Verwende das *present progressive*.

Introduction

What's happening in the picture?

Who is eating in the classroom?

Which of the students are sitting on a desk?

Which student is listening to music?

Who is talking? Who is drawing on the desk?

Who is taking a selfie? Why are the students not sitting at their desks and why are they being so loud?

And what is the teacher doing? Is she just watching the students?

Grammar Help

DIGITAL+ video 32

Mit der Verlaufsform der Gegenwart (***present progressive***) kannst du fragen, was jemand gerade tut oder was gerade passiert. So bildest du Fragen im ***present progressive***:
Form von ***be*** (***am***, ***are***, ***is***) + **ing-Form des Verbs.**

Am I do**ing** my homework? **Are** you do**ing** your homework? **Is** he do**ing** his homework?

Du antwortest auf diese Fragen mit Kurzantworten:
Is she playing with the dog? **Yes, she is. / No, she isn't.**

Bei Fragen mit Fragewort steht das Fragewort am Satzanfang:
What are you do**ing** at the moment?

Language Detective

a

Underline the verbs in the present progressive in the introduction text.
Unterstreiche alle Verben im *present progressive* im Einführungstext.

b

How do you say that in English? Find the verb forms in the introduction text and write them down.
Wie sagt man das auf Englisch? Finde die Verbformen im Einführungstext und schreibe sie auf.

Was passiert gerade? ______________ Wer isst gerade? ______________

Wer redet gerade? ______________ Wer zeichnet gerade? ______________

Welcher Schüler hört gerade Musik? ______________

Was macht die Lehrerin gerade? ______________

So many questions

1

Add the right verb form of *be*. Füge die richtige Verbform von *be* hinzu.

1 ________ you cooking dinner?
2 ________ she playing the piano?
3 ________ we watching TV now?
4 ________ I talking too much?
5 ________ he eating ice cream?
6 ________ they riding their bikes?

More questions

2

Write down questions. Use the *present progressive*.
Schreibe Fragen auf. Verwende das *present progressive*.

1 Mum / do the shopping – what / Mum / buy

Is Mum doing the shopping? What is Mum buying?

2 Dad / cook – what / Dad / cook

____

3 we / go – where / we / go

____

What are they doing?

3

Ask questions. What are the people doing? Add short answers from the box.
Stelle Fragen. Was machen die Menschen gerade? Füge Kurzantworten aus dem Kasten hinzu.

Yes, she is. · No, he isn't. · ~~Yes, they are.~~ · No, they aren't.

1 
2 
3 
4 

1 *Are they eating pizza? – Yes, they are.*
2 ________
3 ________
4 ________

Say it in English

4

How do you say that in English? Write down the questions.
Wie sagt man das auf Englisch? Schreibe die Fragen auf.

1 Wie frage ich, wer gerade arbeitet?

Who is ______

2 Wie frage ich, was gerade passiert?

______

3 Wie frage ich, wohin wir gerade gehen?

______

4 Wie frage ich, wer gerade Musik hört?

______

5 Wie frage ich, was die Kinder gerade spielen?

______

Over to you

What do you ask your family if you want to know what they are doing at the moment? Write down questions. Use the *present progressive*.
Was fragst du deine Familie, wenn du wissen möchtest, was sie gerade machen? Schreibe Fragen auf. Verwende das *present progressive*.

______

______

______

______

______

______

______

Introduction

Lucie: Hey, Paula! How was your holiday?

Paula: My holiday was great, thanks! I was in Spain with my family. We were at the beach. Were you on holiday, too?

Lucie: No, I was at home. But we were very busy! My little brother was outdoors every day. He was with his friends – they were in the park. And I was with Moira all the time. We were at the shopping centre a lot and we were at the swimming pool! It was a lot of fun!

Grammar Help

DIGITAL+ video 33

Abgeschlossene Ereignisse in der Vergangenheit gibt man im ***simple past*** wieder.
Das Verb ***be*** hat zwei Vergangenheitsformen: ***was*** und ***were***.
Für die Verneinung fügst du nach ***was*** bzw. ***were*** ein ***not*** hinzu.

Personalpronomen	Verb	Verneinung	Beispiel
I, he, she, it	**was**	**was not / wasn't**	He **was** in the park. / He **wasn't** in the park.
we, you, they	**were**	**were not / weren't**	We **were** at school. / We **weren't** at school.

Fragen bildest du so:
Were you at Anton's house yesterday? **Was** Ella in Brighton last year?

Language Detective

a

Underline all the past tense forms of the verb *be* in the introduction text.
Unterstreiche alle Vergangenheitsformen des Verbs *be* im Einführungstext.

b

Circle the right form. **Kreise die richtige Form ein.**

1 We **was / were** in Italy last summer.
2 This **was / were** our hotel.
3 It **was / were** very nice.
4 The people **was / were** very friendly.
5 I **was / were** at the beach a lot.
6 We **was / were** in different cities.
7 My mum **was / were** in many museums.
8 My brother **was / were** in lots of shops.

Where were the people last Monday?

1

Complete the sentences with *was, were, wasn't* or *weren't*.
Vervollständige die Sätze mit *was, were, wasn't* oder *weren't*.

1 

2 

3 

4 

5 

6 

1 The girl ________________ at the beach.

2 The boy ________________ at the swimming pool.

3 The girls ________________ at the playground.

4 The man ________________ in the garden.

5 The woman ________________ in the car.

6 The students ________________ in the classroom.

Julia's holidays

2

Write about Julia and her last holidays. **Schreibe über Julia und ihren letzten Urlaub.**

1 at the beach (+) / at the cinema (-) *Julia was at the beach. She wasn't at the cinema.*

2 Spain (+) / Italy (-) ________________

3 weather: good (+) / weather: bad (-) ________________

Many questions

3

Look at number 2 again. Write questions and add short answers.
Sieh dir Aufgabe 2 noch einmal an. Schreibe Fragen und füge Kurzantworten hinzu.

1 *Was Julia at the beach? Yes, she was. Was she at the cinema? No, she wasn't.*

2 ________________

____

3 ________________

____

Say it in English

4

How do you say that in English? Write down the questions.
Wie sagt man das auf Englisch? Schreibe die Fragen auf.

1 Wie sage ich, dass ich gestern im Park war?

2 Wie sage ich, dass das Wetter nicht gut war?

3 Wie sage ich, dass ich nicht im Urlaub war?

4 Wie sage ich, dass ich letztes Wochenende zu Hause war?

5 Wie frage ich, wo mein Lehrer im Urlaub war?

6 Wie frage ich, wann mein Nachbar im Schwimmbad war?

7 Wie frage ich, wie das Wetter in Spanien war?

Over to you

You write an email to your email partner in England. Tell him or her about your last holidays.
Du schreibst deinem E-Mail-Partner / deiner E-Mail Partnerin in England eine E-Mail. Erzähle ihm oder ihr über deine letzten Ferien.